C000176021

WORDS NOT NUMBERS: ASSESSMENT IN ENGLISH

MYRA BARRS

NATIONAL ASSOCIATION OF ADVISERS IN ENGLISH

NATE

Words Not Numbers : Assessment in English

Printed by Short Run Press Ltd., Exeter.
© Myra Barrs July, 1990

ISBN 0901291 24 2

Foreword

No assessment system is merely a matter of technique and know-how. It is always saying something about the assessors and the assessed, and about the world that the assessor is seeking to bring about. It has behind it a view of learning, of the place of the child in the larger world, and of what counts as worthwhile learning.

These are times of great change and pressure for English teachers, not least in the assessment field. Faced by a juggernaut, they have a number of alternatives. They can lie down and give up their professionalism. They can choose defiance and subversion. They can concentrate on the problem of making it work and leave the larger questions alone.

In this paper, Myra Barrs offers a more substantial and in the future a more hopeful way. She analyses how we got here, the better to understand how we might move on. This is no simple task, but we understand more after reading her. She identifies succinctly the nub of good practice, the better for us to hold on to it. She gives us something very difficult to achieve, a perspective of time and place to quieten the buzzing in the ears.

In all this, it is as well to remember that though there has been good assessment practice among English and Language teachers, there has also been too often allegiance to reading tests, comprehension exercises and the use of assessment in one language mode to speak for all. These are all rife in our schools. In this paper, Myra's clear challenge to the TGAT assessment model is also an implicit rebuke to much existing practice and an agenda for some time to come.

David Allen, Chair of NAAE.

Introduction

When I was in the top class at my primary school, one of the most important lessons on the timetable was "Intelligence". I liked Intelligence and I worked hard at it. I particularly enjoyed that type of question which involved cracking a simple code and decoding a "message". This I took to be the first indication of what learning French was going to be like. French was the thing that I most looked forward to at the grammar school (supposing that I made it that far) and I was anxious to know exactly what it was going to entail.

I went in for intense private speculation on this subject and eventually arrived at the theory that French would be a code far more complex and mysterious than any I had yet met, to which, in one's first few days at the grammar school, one would be given the key. Thereafter French lessons would consist simply of practising with this key until one became fluent in its use. When I finally moved to the grammar school and discovered that not only was Intelligence - one of my best subjects - not on the timetable, but that learning French was going to involve learning every word of the language (a patently impossible task), two crucial preconceptions were shattered for me, and I passed my first few weeks there in a state of shock.

I remember too that in that top class we did expect, and were expected, to pass the eleven-plus examination, still called "The Scholarship". A slight edge of uncertainty over this lent a sense of some risk and sickly excitement to the days of the tests, but by and large we in the top class were going to be all right. The children in the second class were less lucky, however, being mostly bound for the secondary modern school at the bottom of the hill - though some of them might slip through the cracks in the system by doing unexpectedly well in the Scholarship. All of this had been decided long ago, whenever it was that we were "streamed", and such a time-honoured system seemed as if it must be right.

The system was good at predicting who would pass the exam, partly, no doubt, because the school had already used the same forms of assessment in streaming and preselecting the children, but also because those children who were expected to pass were given a great deal of intensive coaching in the areas covered by the exam - we in the top class got more Intelligence than anyone else. As the year went by the gap between those in the top class and those in the second class got wider; we were destined to wear different uniforms and walk on opposite sides of the street, and we knew it.

3

When I was invited by the NAAE to write this short book I felt that any account of the assessment of English and Language, at this turning point in the history of the English education system, would have to take a long view of what is happening, and perform a number of different functions. It would have to identify some of the main issues that continually recur in discussions of assessment, and that are particularly relevant to the system that is now being put into place. It would have to situate present events in the context of what has gone before, and try to discern the trends in these historical events. It would have to consider good practice in the assessment of English and Language, and analyse the principles underlying such practice. And finally it would have to confront the emergent national system of assessment, consider its likely effects and its potential problems, and offer some positive suggestions for teachers, advisers and inspectors who are charged with implementing it and yet may need to argue against it. For it is clear that the TGAT system of assessment, as it has now been interpreted by various subject working parties, is becoming an extraordinary incubus -potentially as damaging and as much of a drag on the system, particularly in the primary school, as the eleven-plus ever was.

The shape of the book is therefore as follows. It begins with an "ABC", which foregrounds some of the issues central to any contemporary discussion of assessment. This is followed by a history of assessment in this country, which focuses particularly on assessment since the second world war. Next comes a section on good practice, which includes a survey of important past developments. Lastly, a section on the TGAT model of assessment identifies the kind of problems it is giving rise to, and lists some positive steps that might be taken. There are currently so many developments in the field of assessment, following one another so rapidly, that it is inevitable that some details in this publication will be out of date before it is published. I can only hope that, despite this obvious difficulty, it will nevertheless remain relevant in its essentials for some while yet.

Myra Barrs, May 1990

I should like to thank the following for reading and commenting in detail on the manuscript:

Dave Allen, James Berry, James Britton, Tony Burgess, Pat D'Arcy, Terry Furlong, Keith Kimberley, Ros Moger, Desmond Nuttall, Nick Williams.

4

AN ABC OF ASSESSMENT

- A is for Accountability
- A is for Assessment
- B is for Backwash
- B is for Bias
- C is for Context
- C is for Criterion-Referencing

A IS FOR ACCOUNTABILITY

"I take it that no one claims exclusive rights in this field. Public interest is strong and will be satisfied. It is legitimate. We spend 6 billion a year on education so there will be discussion. If everything is reduced to such phrases as 'educational freedom versus state control' we shall get nowhere." James Callaghan (T.E.S.22.10.76)

"Education, like any other public service, is answerable to the society which it serves, and which pays for it." Education in Schools, A consultative document HMSO 1977

It was in the 1970s, at around the time of James Callaghan's Ruskin speech, signalling the beginning of the so-called 'Great Debate', that the term 'accountability' began to be heard with any frequency in the UK, though it was already familiar in the USA. There may have been many reasons for the acountability movement, from a growing distrust of professionalism, to a general decline in consensual values, but the main reasons publicly given for the need for greater accountability were generally three: the need to ensure that education was giving value for the money that was being spent on it; a concern about standards; and a feeling that the content of the curriculum had become too exclusively the concern of professionals.

Economic concerns had long been expressed in the USA. Ernest House(1978) described how, in the mid-sixties, systems analysts were brought into the Department of Health, Education and Welfare. "Systems analysis relates a few quantitative outcome variables like test scores to different programs. That program is best which can raise test scores highest for the lowest cost." Unfortunately, according to House, the fact that federally-funded programs could not be shown to have resulted in any improvement in test scores under this kind of input-output model led to pressures to cut education budgets.

The same issue of cost-effectiveness is still stressed by Archie Lapointe, Director of the NAEP (National Assessment of Educational Progress) - the equivalent of the APU:

"The states and the Federal Government have consistently increased the expenditure for education during the past twenty years. Local communities, states and the Federal Government have invested large sums of money for general and specific programs to improve certain aspects of the system. Media commentators, the legislators and parents want to know what has happened as a result of these expenditures and efforts and why is the current concern over the condition of education so serious. What has the American public gotten for its money? One natural response to this query is to test children, teachers and the system and find out the current status." (1986)

The spread of management techniques on the American model has undoubtedly contributed to pressures to measure the effectiveness of the education system in the UK.

Concern about standards has been a recurring feature of public discussion of education in recent years. The Bullock Report discussed these concerns at length, and the APU was its suggested means of satisfying them. Hypotheses about whether standards are falling or rising are notoriously difficult to substantiate but, as Stuart Maclure has pointed out, this has never deterred anybody since "there is a fall-back position for the protagonists of dissatisfaction: if standards are not actually falling they are not high enough to meet the rising demands of modern life." (1978) There are complex and technical arguments to be had about standards which involve the problems of measuring achievement over time: "The seeming precision and accuracy of published quantitative data mask the difficulty of adequately selecting or determining and representing the range of criteria which truly reflect educational standards." (Cohen, 1987) But public debate deals with the issue in much more simplistic terms than these.

However, it was the move to limit the power of professionals and to gain greater central control over the 'secret garden' of the curriculum which was unquestionably one of the most important subtexts of Callaghan's Ruskin speech. This continued to be the major motive force behind a series of government initiatives - whatever government was in power - which culminated in the introduction of the Education Reform Act in 1988.

Throughout the period since 1976 there has also been legislation to ensure that schools provide full information for parents, and to give parents

6

increased opportunities to participate in schools. Schools are, above all, accountable to children and their parents and therefore, as John Nisbet says "Ultimately, accountability should be concerned with the school reporting to the parent. There is a danger however that a highly sophisticated system, designed to suit the requirements of technocrats and planners, may neglect the basic concerns of the private citizen." Recent discussions about the level of detail at which children's achievements in the National Curriculum will be reported to parents illustrate this point.

Public demands for accountability could be satisfied by other means than the assessment of individual pupils. The hunt is on, indeed, for other means, "performance indicators" being the latest fashionable solution. More sophisticated methods could include "sampling" the system in a variety of more qualitative ways, at all levels, from that of the experiences available to individual pupils, to that of the effectiveness of an LEA. Such approaches might not, however, yield numerical results, and this fact alone is likely to make them unpopular with administrators intent on measurement.

A IS FOR ASSESSMENT

"There can be little doubt that summative assessment, which can be defined simply as assessment of the outcomes of education for the purpose of reporting or certification, dominates the educational psyche of assessment." (Harry Black, 1986)

After TGAT we are all familiar with the definition of the four purposes which national assessment would have to serve: formative, diagnostic, summative, and evaluative. It should be remembered that the TGAT report stated that assessment might serve more than one of these purposes, and expressed the view that the basis of a national system should be essentially formative. True formative assessment can be a very positive influence on teaching and learning. It provides a visible record of development which can help children and teachers, and can be the basis for a fruitful dialogue with parents. Moreover the skills which teachers can develop through the experience of ongoing formative assessment can make them more effective teachers.

Another classic definition of assessment was given by Macintosh and Hale, who defined six purposes of assessment: 1. diagnosis 2. evaluation

3. guidance   4. grading   5. selection   6. prediction (monitoring). The problem is that though all these purposes are theoretically part of any system, in practice the more public and accountability-oriented purposes of assessment - summative assessment for the purposes of selection and prediction (5 and 6) - always tend to dominate the system. Whenever an assessment is expressed in terms of a score, grade, or figure of any kind, there is always the danger that this measure will take on a life of its own. "There is a strong tendency for quantitative data to overwhelm other forms of information. Test scores are easy to feature in newspaper headlines and they have an appeal difficult to resist." (House, 1978) Moreover, when assessment is expressed numerically this tends to encourage the belief that those things which cannot be reduced to numbers do not really count. Throughout the world in recent years there has been a demand for easily understood measures of education, and the measures used for this purpose have often been seriously reductive.

In these circumstances, TGAT's recommendation that all assessment before the age of sixteen should be seen as essentially formative looks naive, especially in view of the fact that they were simultaneously recommending that children should be given grades on a scale of 1 to 10 at ages 7, 11, 14 and 16, and that results at 11 and above should be published. Desmond Nuttall believes that "You cannot combine formative, summative and evaluative purposes and expect them all to function unaffected by each other." (Nuttall 1989) It seems clear, given previous experience, that the monitoring or evaluative function of the national system is likely to predominate, and that TGAT's idea of assessment as "the servant, not the master, of the curriculum" will come to appear a rhetorical flourish.

Discussions of assessment also need to include a consideration of what is going to be assessed. It is clear that in systems where assessment is important, those subjects and aspects of achievement which come within the framework of assessment will have a higher status than those which do not. The Hargreaves Report (1984) identified one of the problems of secondary education as its narrow focus on the academic skills which came within the scope of conventional assessment. The Report saw an urgent need to widen the accepted definition of achievement, and named four aspects of achievement that it would be important to recognise and include in a broad programme of assessment. They included problem-solving skills, motivation and commitment, and the kind of propositional knowledge tested by external written examinations.

The Attainment Targets of the National Curriculum, however, are designed to assess only "knowledge, skills, and understanding" in each

8

subject area. The TGAT Report specifically excluded the assessment of attitudes from the new national system, while the creation of a three tier curriculum in which there are core subjects, foundation subjects, and others, has seriously marginalised important areas of experience.

B IS FOR BACKWASH

County Students improve CAP Scores
Teaching to the Test Credited with Improvement in Basic Skills

Students in San Diego County public schools scored better this year on every phase of the state's annual battery of basic skills tests, especially in districts gearing their curriculum to fit the exams, results showed.
...The lesson many school districts have drawn from the CAP, according to superintendents, is that if a school system wants to score high it should 'teach to the test'. 'That doesn't mean they are cheating' said Pierson. 'But they are moulding their curriculum to fit what the CAP tests.'
...South Bay Union Superintendent Peter Hartman said his district deliberately focuses its curriculum at the material covered in the CAP, 'skills which every school system thinks are important anyway'.

(San Diego Union, California, 2.12.82, quoted in Gipps et al, 1983)

Just as summative assessment for the purposes of selection and for accountability always tends to dominate thinking and practice in relation to assessment, so there is always the danger that it will come to dominate the school curriculum. The Californian example above is quoted by Gipps to show how, in a situation where test scores are used for monitoring purposes, teaching to the test can dominate the curriculum - "The curriculum is openly admitted to be geared, moulded, focused and remodelled upon the test." (Gipps et al., 1983)

There is, of course, plenty of experience to confirm this in the UK. The 11 plus was acknowledged to have dominated and limited the curriculum in the last years of the junior school over a long period; this indeed was one of the strongest criticsms of the exam. It is true that Gipps et al. found that in certain circumstances some of the LEA educationalists they interviewed **welcomed** backwash effects; LEA advisers, for instance, sometimes saw the APU maths and science assessments as having had a beneficial influence on teaching in schools. But such 'positive backwash' seems to be rare compared with the more numerous examples of narrowing curriculum towards what is to be tested, at the expense of other untested areas. Eisner reports that in the USA "About seventy to eighty five per cent of all of the

9

time allocated for instructional purposes in elementary schools is devoted to the teaching of the three Rs. The arts, by contrast, secure from two to four per cent of instructional time per week." (Eisner, 1985)

The danger that tests will bring about a narrowing of curriculum also carries with it the likelihood that they will, in the long run, actually lower standards rather than raise them (which is often the expectation). A broad and rich curriculum is more likely to develop children's abilities than one which is focused on the narrow range of skills assessable through standardised tests. Nor will criterion-referenced assessment necessarily be more positive in its effects than norm-referencing in this respect. "Much of the evidence from other countries suggests that attainment targets when designed for a whole population of school pupils of a given age, are more likely to decrease expectations, have a harmful restricting influence on teaching approaches, and generally lower educational standards rather than raising them." (Murphy and Torrance,1988)

B IS FOR BIAS

"TGAT paid lipservice to bias in assessment but didn't grapple with its true nature." (Desmond Nuttall, 1989)

One of the problems of assessment is that it is hard to achieve culture or gender fair assessment. Bias may enter the assessment process by many doors.

First, and most obviously, the **content** of assessment may be such that it favours children with a particular set of past experiences. This is clearly true of assessment that tests detailed knowledge of any kind, but may also apply to assessments with a less obvious cultural or experiential content. This is one of the factors that has led to an increasing distrust of standardised IQ tests in the United States, where court cases have, in some places, confirmed evidence of discrimination in the tests (Gupta and Coxhead, 1988).

Secondly, the **technology** of the assessment may favour certain groups. The Equal Opportunities Commission, in their evidence to TGAT for instance (TGAT Appendix F), quoted research to show that multiple choice testing favours boys. Desmond Nuttall summarises some of the research which led to this conclusion:
"Patricia Murphy has shown, from her work for the Assessment of Performance Unit, how a problem can be perceived in different ways by

10

boys and girls. Boys tend to abstract the problem from the context while girls attend to the totality of the problem context including what I, as a male, might describe as extraneous and irrelevant cues. She surmises that it is perhaps this characteristic of girls that makes them do less well than boys in multiple-choice tests, when the reader is bombarded with irrelevant and often erroneous information." (Nuttall 1989)

Thirdly, the **context** of the assessment may favour particular groups, or may be particularly intimidating or disadvantaging for other groups. Labov's classic study, **The Logic of Non-standard English** offers one account of how, in a formal testing situation with a white interviewer, a black child can adopt 'defensive, monosyllabic behaviour'. In the same paper Labov shows how a deliberately informal setting and a shift in the social situation can transform a 'non-verbal' child into a lively and talkative one.

Finally, the **interpretation** of the assessment may be biased.
"Even when we use a standardised objective test we must still make many personal assessments, consciously or unconsciously. We must assess the reliability of our use of the test, the validity of the inferences we make from the results, and assessments of what to do with the results, and how to alter our teaching in their light." (Stibbs, 1981). It is clear that many apparently objective measures involve interpretation and the exercise of personal judgement. Attitudes may affect the way that assessments are carried out, or the reading of the result. Gipps et al found that teachers tended to use test results to confirm their own existing impressions, and sometimes took no notice of a result which did not agree with their own observations.

C IS FOR CONTEXT

"When I was a student at Lawson Elementary School during the 1940s I was expected, as were all of my classmates, to take a handwriting test on a yearly basis. Each year from grade 3 on the teacher would write on the blackboard in her finest cursive form the following: "This is a sample of my handwriting on January 24, 1943. If it is not as good as it should be for a student of my age and grade, I will try with my teacher's help to improve by this time next year."
I remember vividly sitting on the hard oak seat attached to a desk screwed into the floor, eight deep in rows of six. The white, slick, lined paper was before me with the blue-black watery ink at my right as I sat with scratchy pen in hand. Oh, how I worked! To copy those two sentences in my best hand was a venture as difficult as crossing the Niagara on a high wire. After twenty minutes of pain I was through - in my best hand. But what I turned in to the teacher was no more a sample of my

11

handwriting than it was of the man in the moon's. If my teachers wanted to know how I wrote, all they had to do was to look at what I was writing on any school day."
(Eisner, 1985)

One of the most persistent criticisms of external assessment - both in the form of public exams and standardised tests - has been that it sets up artificial contexts, often very minimal ones, and does not succeed in sampling a child's normal level of work. The history of examining in English over the last thirty years has shown a consistent trend towards coursework-based forms of assessment, in which pupils' achievements can be assessed in normal classroom contexts. By implication, arguments against external assessments have pointed to the vacuum within which external assessors are operating; lacking a context for their assessments they are in no position to know whether their judgements are accurate in relation to a student's normal performance.

On the whole, these arguments about context have been accepted by the assessment community, and instruments for external assessment have increasingly reflected a desire to simulate, as far as possible, normal classroom tasks and contexts. The APU made noticeable attempts to simulate classroom reading and writing tasks in their surveys of language performance, while some recent reading tests have gone a long way towards imitating real reading experiences, by presenting tests in the form of colourful illustrated booklets, containing complete stories.

One problem introduced by this tendency is that, the more external assessment strives to provide naturalistic contexts for assessment and to simulate real school learning situations, the more invasive it becomes in terms of time. 'Cheap and nasty' standardised tests were soon over with, even if their results were not, but these more ambitious naturalistic assessments require children and teachers to behave as they would behave in normal classroom situations, so that individual assessments can take a considerable time. The furthest development of this softer, but more invasive kind of external assessment is likely to be seen in the SATs.

C IS FOR CRITERION-REFERENCING

"Criterion-referencing is more about the curriculum than it is about assessment."
(Desmond Nuttall, 1990)

There is a clear shift in assessment at every level now away from psychological and psychometric approaches, and towards educational measurement. This shift has taken place both within the assessment community, and at a political level. Keith Joseph's speech to the North of England Conference in 1984 was an important signal of this change of tack. "We should move towards a greater degree of criterion-referencing in these (16+) examinations and away from norm-referencing. The existing system tells us a great deal about relative standards between different candidates. It tells us much less about absolute standards. We lack clear definitions of the level of knowledge and performance expected from candidates for the award of particular grades. We need a reasonable assurance that pupils obtaining a particular grade will know certain things and possess certain skills or have achieved a certain competence."

Criterion-referenced testing is widely seen as a fairer, more effective, and more pupil-and-teacher-friendly kind of assessment than norm-referenced testing. This is partly because we are all very familiar with criterion-referenced assessment since many informal tests set by teachers come within this category. In the USA, where norm-referenced assessment has had such a pervasive and negative effect on schools, criterion-referencing may look like a very big step forward. ("With NRSTs driving the important decision making, we limit excellence to under 16% of the school population. If we dared to drive educational decision making with CRTs as integral parts of instruction, we might be so efficient that 99% of the school population would achieve excellence." (Cohen, 1988)

Any kind of assessment, even the most informal, must obviously relate to some criteria. The sort of broad, informing criteria that help teachers as they form a judgement of a pupil's work are, however, very different from the sort of detailed testable criteria that assessment experts generally have in mind when they refer to criterion-referencing. And criteria closely tied to grades or levels, as in the model of assessment adopted for the national curriculum, represent the worst of both worlds (norm-referencing and criterion-referencing) for they constrain judgement rather than supporting it, and do not allow work to be assessed as a whole on its own terms.

There are important questions to be asked about the use of criterion-referenced assessments across the whole curriculum and for summative purposes, and about what will happen once there is pressure to establish homogeneity and parity across CR tests. At the moment the technology of criterion-referenced assessment is in its infancy, and many traditional psychometric approaches used to standardise norm-referenced assessment are simply not applicable to CRTs.

This state of affairs is not likely to last, as Harry Black has pointed out:
"It could well be that we will witness, over the next few years, a psychometric bandwagon in the technology of criterion-referenced assessment design. The focus will almost certainly be on the large-scale domains which have the greatest appeal to examination board interests. It is highly likely, therefore, that workers in this field will place considerable emphasis on issues such as the statistical procedures appropriate to manipulate 'observed' scores into 'true' scores, the complex issue of optimum test length and on the use of procedures such as item response theory to choose option test items." (Black, 1986)

It is interesting that government should be opting for criterion-referenced assessment on such a large scale when it seems so unsuited to the sorts of summative purposes that dominate thinking about assessment at a political level. The only plausible explanation of this shift is that criterion-referenced assessment involves a much sharper definition of what is to be learnt than is the case with norm-referenced assessment. The move to criterion-referenced assessment, where the criteria are laid down at national level, thus enables central government to exert maximum control over the content of the curriculum, something which has been a DES aim for some time.

Criterion-referencing is inextricably linked with the educational objectives movement, which has been such a feature of education in the USA for the past thirty years. Popham, an American assessment expert and proponent of educational objectives, states the relationship as follows:
"Any educational evaluator who seriously believes that objectives-achievement ought to be a key element in the evaluation of educational programs must reckon with a major task, namely, determining whether objectives have, in fact, been achieved....it is generally accepted that, for the purposes of educational evaluation, criterion-referenced tests are to be strongly preferred over their norm - referenced counterparts." (Popham, 1987)

Popham quotes a classic paper by Robert Glaser (Glaser 1963) on this subject which first demonstrated that, whereas norm-referenced measures only give relative interpretations, criterion-referenced measures give absolute interpretations "such as whether an examinee could master a well defined set of criterion behaviours." The parallels here with Sir Keith Joseph's speech are clear.

14

But criterion-referenced assessment is not all going to be plain sailing. The experience of trying to develop grade-related criteria at GCSE seems to have been an expensive failure. The problem about all criterion-referencing is the level of detail at which criteria have to be specified in order to offer an adequate description of what constitutes a satisfactory performance. This produces unwieldy lists of descriptors. A related problem is that there is often a tendency to specify what is specifiable, and thus to leave out more important but indefinable criteria, or in Desmond Nuttall's words: "...there is a great danger of fragmentation into discrete objectives, often low level because they are the easiest to specify, with the loss of high level and integrating objectives." (Nuttall, 1990)

Popham, who is a major figure in the objectives field, acknowledges the same problem in the development of behavioural objectives. He analyses it as "the common tendency to frame behavioural objectives so that they focus on smaller and more specific segments of learner postinstruction behaviour. The net effect of such hyperspecificity is that the objectives formulator ends up with a plethora of picayune outcomes .... if decision-makers were quite literally overwhelmed with lengthy lists of behavioural objectives, how could they meaningfully focus on whether such objectives were achieved?" (Popham 1987) His solution to this dilemma is to "coalesce small-scope behaviours under larger, albeit still measurable behavioural rubrics." But the development of such "broad-scope measurable objectives" may prove more difficult than he acknowledges. Popham's observations are interesting in the light of the experience of the National Curriculum, and the continuing proliferation of statements of attainment.

A consideration of this whole history explains quite clearly why there has been such confusion between Programmes of Study and Attainment Targets in English, and so much discussion about which should drive the curriculum and inform planning. Though the rhetoric of the National Curriculum depicts PoS as the programme for the curriculum while presenting ATs as the framework for assessment only, even a brief consideration of criterion-referenced assessment shows that this kind of assessment is designed to impact on curriculum, and is implicitly linked to educational objectives. The ATs, therefore, constitute an alternative programme for the curriculum - and the only one which will be subject to assessment. This was made starkly clear in the National Curriculum for Maths and Science, where the Programmes of Study and the Attainment Targets are more or less identical, and also in the way in which the second Cox Report, under pressure from the DES, redrew the Programmes of Study to mirror more exactly the words of the Statements of Attainment.

15

A SHORT HISTORY OF ASSESSMENT

A TRADITION OF SELECTION

Although definitions of assessment suggest a wide range of purposes for assessment (formative, diagnostic, summative etc), traditionally, public assessment in Britain has taken place for the purposes of selection. At primary level, testing began to be used to any considerable extent in the 1930s, when about 5% of the places in grammar schools were designated as 'free' places and were open to competition. IQ ('ability') and English and Arithmetic ('attainment') tests were the means chosen for selecting to these places.

After the war, the 1945 Act and the establishment of a tripartite system meant that IQ tests (and their successors, verbal reasoning tests) came to be widely used for selection purposes, along with English and Arithmetic tests, in LEAs throughout England and Wales until this 11+ testing reached its peak in 1960. In the early part of this period, testing was seen as a fair way of identifying able children and allocating them to scarce places, but increasingly throughout the period it was shown that the "innate" ability that IQ tests was believed to measure was decidedly susceptible to coaching. There was also criticism of the "self-fulfilling prophecy" effect of the tests.

The origins of the GCE exams also lay in selection procedures. At the end of the nineteenth century universities were setting their own entrance exams; in 1918 these separate procedures were rationalised into the School Certificate and the Higher School Certificate. These exams survived until 1950, when they were replaced by the GCE O and A levels. The university exam boards continued to administer these examinations. Though suitable as a means of selection for higher education, they were only ever designed to serve a minority of the age group - 20-30% in the case of O Level - and this left the great majority of the population with no access to qualifications at sixteen.

The selection function of assessment in Britain has always been a dominating factor and has made the reform of assessment and examining hard to achieve. In recent years it has led to contradictory and illogical demands on schools. For instance, it has been seen (rightly) as scandalous that large numbers of school leavers have few qualifications, yet moves to create assessment systems which would accommodate a broader population (CSE, GCSE) have been resisted or criticised. Such an essentially unfair and irrational situation has been hard to circumvent. Secondary English teachers have tended to do so by entering large numbers of pupils for exams not designed to take them, and by dint of using Mode 3 arrangements and continuous assessment have often helped their students to succeed. But successes of this kind have not always been welcomed and have often been seen as evidence of a lowering of standards. The idea of selection is so ingrained in the system that fresh thinking about assessment is hard to achieve.

THE ROLE OF LANGUAGE IN ASSESSMENT

In these selection procedures, English, or language, has often played a particularly prominent role. Verbal ability has proved to be a good long-term predictor of school achievement, so tests which claim to discriminate on the basis of verbal intelligence, or verbal reasoning, have had a special place in testing programmes. This was clearly shown during the decline in testing which took place in the 1960s; in many LEAs the VR test was the only test which survived the general withering away of testing programmes.

Similarly, when testing for monitoring purposes swept the country towards the end of the 1970s, it was reading tests that were most commonly chosen to monitor school performance. Since most tests are based on old-fashioned models of reading, with an emphasis on decoding, this has sometimes had an unfortunate backwash effect on practice - but it has also led to a more critical attitude to testing, since teachers who are well-informed about reading theory are in a position to evaluate the tests. Both reading tests and VR tests are standardised norm-referenced tests, and this fact has tended to shape expectations about children's performance.

NORM REFERENCING

Norm-referenced testing is based on the notion that ability is distributed, in normal populations, on a normal distribution curve, and that whereas most people (68%) will fall into a broad middle band, there will be an exceptional 16% at the top of the curve, balanced by a below-average 16% at the bottom. This psychometric concept is not, however, appropriate to use when describing the outcomes of learning, and norm-referenced tests are more useful for discriminating between people than they are for assessing learning. Because of this, they have been heavily used to support selective practices.

Public examination results are also norm-referenced; the results are plotted on a curve with the consequence that a percentage of the candidates always fail or are unclassified. As well as supporting the selective function, this practice also maintains 'standards'; it ensures that a constant percentage of candidates achieve excellence. The weakness of this argument is that it deals only in percentages; an individual 'borderline' candidate might have achieved a different grade for the same performance in another year when the average performance was higher, or lower. It will be apparent from this that talk of 'standards' is heavily influenced by psychometric thinking, and by the highly selective emphasis of the whole English system.

The strong tradition of norm-referenced testing also tends to affect people's general thinking, and to foster the belief that humanity is really divided into unchanging bands of ability. It can be seen as having had a considerable influence on expectations: "The growing obsession with NRSTs (norm-referenced standardised tests) over the last sixty years has a lot of people convinced that only a few students will ever be excellent, an equal number will fail, and the largest number will be mediocre." (Cohen, 1988)

THE GROWTH OF THE COMPREHENSIVE SECTOR

It is impossible to consider the changing role of assessment in the mid-century without reference to the ending of selection for secondary schools. The growth of the comprehensive sector affected assessment practices in both primary and secondary schools. It made assessment for selection unnecessary at the top of the primary school, and it created the need for a common system of assessment for the comprehensive school. But comprehensivisation took place over a very long period - over twenty years - and against a background of considerable resistance from an educational and social establishment which could not conceive how selection could be ended without a decline in standards.

One of the most vocal centres of resistance were the Black Papers in Education, edited initially by two English Literature academics - C. B. Cox and A.E.Dyson, of Manchester University - and then by C. B. Cox and Rhodes Boyson, a headteacher who became a Conservative politician. The early contributors included Angus Maude, Kingsley Amis, H.J.Eysenck and Cyril Burt. The Black Papers attacked what they called the "progressive collapse of education" at all levels of the system from infant school to university. Their theme was always that rampant egalitarianism in education was threatening the whole fabric of society:
"We **need** first-class surgeons, engineers, scientists, mathematicians, lawyers and scholars, and these can only show up through a system of elitist training and competitive exams." (Editorial, Black Paper Two)

"We cannot expect highly qualified graduates...to be prepared to spend half or more of their time on non-talented pupils (in comprehensive schools)." ("Comprehensive Disaster" R.R.Pedley, Black Paper One) The Black Papers were being written during a period when a certain amount of expansion was taking place in higher education as a consequence of the Robbins Report. Though British higher education was recognised as being more exclusive than that in any other European country any widening of access was seen as dilution by the Black Paper commentators. Kingsley Amis coined the saying that 'more means worse'.

The slow and disorganised growth of the comprehensive sector meant that assessment arrangements lagged far behind what was needed. Until 1965 when the CSE was created to extend the target group for public examinations, secondary modern and early comprehensive schools got by with a patchwork of examination arrangements for their pupils. But ironically in the same year which established a dual system of examining, the DES circular 10/65 encouraged LEAs towards comprehensive reorganisation. It was not until five years later, in 1970, that the Schools Council called for the establishment of a common system of examining, a recommendation which took nearly twenty years to come to fruition.

THE TREND OF READING STANDARDS

Throughout the 1960s the assessment scene in primary schools was patchy. Though testing programmes were in decline - verbal reasoning tests often surviving as the best predictor of 'aptitude' for schooling - in many places tests were retained. Sometimes this was to aid selection to an unreorganised secondary sector, but sometimes a programme remained in force because it helped comprehensive secondary schools to assign their intake to streams - or in other words it supported internal selection. Test scores, particularly reading test scores, were also used in some authorities to decide on the deployment of remedial help, or on the allocation of resources, which were sometimes directed to schools with low scores. Heads used test scores to argue for better staffing or for a larger share of 'compensatory' funds.

But in the early 1970s a growing national preoccupation with standards flared to alarm when, in 1972, a national survey carried out by the NFER as one of a series of surveys since the second world war, showed an apparent decline in reading standards since the previous survey in 1964. It was the publication of this survey, called "The Trend in Reading Standards", which led Margaret Thatcher, then Secretary of State for Education, to set up a Committee of Inquiry into the teaching of English, the Bullock Committee.

The Bullock Committee tried hard to allay fears about national trends. The first chapters of its Report were a carefully argued analysis of attitudes, standards, and the reality of practice in the schools, as opposed to impressionistic evidence. It made an important contribution to an objective assessment of English teaching practice in its survey, the results of which should have been enough to convince anybody that 'a climate of unchecked creativity' was far from being the norm in the nation's schools. The Report also made detailed criticisms of the Watts-Vernon reading test, which had provided much of the data for the NFER survey, both on psychometric grounds and on educational grounds ("We do not regard these tests as adequate measures of reading ability. What they measure is a narrow aspect of silent reading comprehension.")

But by the time the Bullock Report was published in 1975, the national mood had already moved on. Despite the fact that there had been a change of government, 'standards' were still preoccupying politicians. In 1976 the then prime minister, James Callaghan, made his Ruskin College speech launching a so-called 'Great Debate' on education, a kind of national stock-taking. Following this, in the late seventies, the extent of LEA testing of reading increased dramatically. Despite the Bullock Committee's arguments against blanket testing and in favour of a national monitoring system based on regular light sampling (the APU), local politicians wanted their own means of monitoring standards, and they chose reading test scores as the source of information. The commonest test chosen for this purpose was the Young's Group Reading Test; it is doubtful whether the Bullock Committee would have regarded this test as "an adequate measure of reading ability".

THE ASSESSMENT OF PERFORMANCE UNIT

The Assessment of Performance Unit came into being partly in response to a growing interest in monitoring and in the evaluation of the education system, partly as a means of keeping track of national standards that would avoid the kind of moral panic generated by the 1972 NFER Survey, and partly as a first move towards greater DES control over the curriculum. Though it was originally set up as an offshoot of the Educational Disadvantage Unit, with a brief of identifying the incidence of under-achievement, it soon moved centre stage and its role became clearly identified as that of monitoring national standards. The model for the APU was clearly the NAEP (National Assessment of Educational Performance) in the USA; three DES-sponsored teams were sent to the USA in the late seventies to keep an eye on the experience of the NAEP (Burstall and Kay in 1976, Black and Marjoram in 1978, and Pring and Selby in 1979).

The APU adopted the NAEP method of matrix sampling and adhered to a principle of light sampling throughout its operations. In this way, it allayed some of the fears that it might become a full-blown national assessment programme, and a way of measuring the performance of schools and teachers as well as children. But the NFER's plan to use the model of APU tests to create "item banks" for LEAs to draw on (LEASIB), in a way which would enable LEA testing to be directly linked into national norms, obviously opened a back-door route to large scale national assessment.

The plans for LEASIB foundered on the technical problems that the NFER encountered with their preferred way of measuring achievement over time - the Rasch model, or latent trait analysis. This method assumed that items in a bank could be classed in order of difficulty in relation to a single ability "trait", for instance a particular reading skill, and replaced by items of the same level of difficulty when they became obviously dated. This was always a controversial model of assessment and criticisms of it (notably by Goldstein (1979) and Nuttall (1980) led to its virtual abandonment by the early eighties. Measurement of educational performance over time is an intractable problem, because the whole context of the measurement is constantly changing, and so of course are the measures themselves, for "what is ostensibly the same measure, relied upon as an unchanging yardstick, is in reality slowly changing its nature" (Nuttall,1986). The most superficial examination of assessment instruments from forty or fifty years ago will confirm this.

In the event, the APU did not make much impression on teachers, the public or politicians. "The impact of published reports, particularly on teachers, has been poor." (Gipps, 1986) APU reports were low-key, and framed in such a way that they were hard to summarise in a snappy way in newspapers. They were not the stuff of headlines. Though this reassured the teaching profession, it did not help to establish the APU as the watchdog for standards that it was intended to be, and more thought needed to have been given to the communication of the Unit's findings if it was going to fulfil accountability demands. Burstall and Kay had foreseen this problem in their report on their visit to America and actually ended the report with the words "The effective communication of the APU's findings through a variety of channels to a variety of audiences may prove one of its most difficult tasks." (Burstall and Kay, 1978)

But the APU did break new ground as far as techniques of assessment were concerned. The Unit took the difficult task of assessing oracy seriously, while their writing and reading assessments went some way to meeting professional criticisms of much previous assessment in language. Above all, in language, the assessment techniques used were not 'objective' machine-scored methods, but the kind of assessments that had been developed in Mode Three CSE and GCE examinations, involving multiple marking and cross-moderating. The range and variety of texts in both the writing and the reading assessments were wide, and carefully simulated contexts were provided for reading and writing tasks. Though not exciting, these assessments thus avoided some of the worst pitfalls of assessment in this aspect of curriculum. The data collected through the APU surveys were analysed carefully and did provide some information about what children of 11 and 14 could do - information which was later fed to the Cox Working Group to help them in their task of fixing 'levels of attainment'. (No such data, it should be noted, existed for 7 year olds).

In Science, the approach to assessment was far more controversial since it proved impossible to test scientific ability without reference to content. The APU science assessments for age 11, for instance, laid down thirty one 'concept statements' which were assumed in the assessments for eleven year olds, and beyond this provided six detailed lists of further concepts which, taken together, virtually defined a science teaching programme from the top of the junior school up to age 16. This objectives-based approach obviously prefigures the attainment statements of the National Curriculum.

The more covert purpose of the APU had undoubtedly been to achieve a greater measure of central control of curriculum by the backwash effects from the assessment. APU Reports acknowledge the inevitability of this process. ("It must be accepted that assessment procedures may transmit messages to teachers about curricular priorities" Language Performance, APU 1978). And insofar as the APU was a stalking horse for a centralised curriculum, as well as a national assessment system, the Education Reform Act of 1988 made it redundant.

REDEFINING THE AGENDA OF ASSESSMENT

The rapid establishment of the APU had been one indication of the hotting up of the accountability climate in the UK; others were the explosion of LEA testing programmes and pressure for the publication of school examination results (made law by the Education Act of 1980) and inspection reports. The changing role of LEA advisers and the increasing emphasis on inspection and monitoring were further obvious indicators. It was in this climate of a much more politicised approach to assessment that assessment experts became more aware of the uses to which their work was being put. The predominantly psychometric tradition of educational assessment in Britain began to be challenged. A passage from a recent book sums up the connections that some workers in the field began to make at this time: "In the same way that, for years, intelligence tests restricted the view of human intelligence, prominent assessment methods (as used in public examinations) have tended to distort concepts of educational achievement. Indeed, one can go even further in claiming a strong link between the two movements. Much of the development work, in the area of educational assessment, conducted by the public examination boards, has been influenced by psychometric concepts and ideas borrowed directly from the same psychologists who promoted the development of intelligence tests in the early part of this century. The traditional presentation of results in the form of single letter (or number) grades, and the aggregation of such grades, by many users, to give an overall estimate of an individual's achievements (and potential), reflects much of the former thinking of psychologists such as Burt and Spearman who believed in a basic (largely inherited) single trait of mental ability that could be used to explain most, if not all, human behaviour." (Murphy and Torrance, 1988)

Patricia Broadfoot's book, *Assessment, Schools and Society* was an influential sociological study of assessment practices. Broadfoot argued that assessors had taken too little account of the social effects of their work: "Educational assessment, perhaps more than any other aspect of education, has suffered the thraldom of 'methodological empiricism' in which questions of technique have effectively predominated over the more fundamental issue of its effects".

ACCOUNTABILITY IN AMERICA

Assessment experts in this country were also aware of the experience in the USA, where the accountability movement had begun a good deal earlier, and testing was rife. Educational measurement there was closely linked to the behavioural objectives movement, which was rooted in Skinnerian behaviourist psychology. Teachers were being required to analyse desired learning 'outcomes' into clear discrete objectives, and to use these as the focus of their teaching programmes, measuring the results at the end of the course. The very simplicity of this kind of model made it attractive to administrators and paymasters, and it had clear analogies with developments in scientific management in industry. But like all atomistic models of learning, it had to leave out some of the most subtle and important qualities that contributed to learning, and which were often unspecifiable and unmeasurable in the terms required. It also ignored the complex interrelationships between different abilities, and the way in which the learner was able to control and orchestrate different kinds of skills and knowledge. This meant that it was an essentially reductive model which, over time, tended to depress expectations and lower achievement.

From 1975 there was a trend in many States towards "minimum competency" testing, where "baselines" of specified minimum level of knowledge had to be achieved by each student, who would be tested at a number of different points in her/his school career. Children who did not achieve at this minimum level would be held back to repeat the year, or channelled into remedial programmes. But, again, the minimum competency movement proved to be damaging in its long term effects, since it focused attention on the lowest level of achievement required, and did nothing to encourage teachers or students to think beyond the baselines.

Testing proliferated. Though the work of the NAEP had been intended to reduce the need for wider testing it seemed instead to stimulate it (a parallel result to that experienced in the UK after the setting up of the APU). State testing programmes sprang up, some of them very extensive. Schools were given lengthy computer printouts of their results, some of them showing each student's performance on each item in relation to all other students in the system, as well as each school's rank order based on these scores. There were attempts to use the results of tests as a yardstick for the evaluation, promotion and dismissal of teachers.

By the late eighties, however, testing programmes seemed to have peaked and there are now moves in some states to get rid of testing in the lower grades. One reason for this is that it is now beginning to be more generally perceived that the effects of this kind of testing may have been to narrow the curriculum and depress achievement. Commentators have suggested that the reason why the USA shows up so badly in international assessment is because its whole schooling system and curriculum is so driven by norm-referenced tests. But most assessment in America is still firmly in the hands of technicians, and there are only very tentative moves towards the kinds of educational (as opposed to psychological) forms of assessment that have been developing in the UK. However, the NAEP is leading the way in investigating alternative forms of assessment (such as the 'portfolio', or folder, assessment of writing) and has begun to look at ways of assessing what are termed 'higher order' objectives.

TWO DISTINCT TRENDS

Two clear trends have marked developments in assessment in the UK over the last twenty years. On the one hand, there have been very positive developments in secondary school examinations and a growth, too, in forms of continuous assessment which involve children, and sometimes parents, and which are designed to take a broad view of educational achievement. One the other hand, there has been continued pressure for greater accountability through testing and other forms of assessment, culminating in the National Curriculum and its assessment system, which lays down a very tight specification indeed for the work of schools. These two trends have, however, one thing in common, which is a move away from norm-referenced measures of 'ability' and towards criterion-referenced measures of attainments or achievement.

At secondary level, there has been a movement towards continuous assessment and coursework, in place of external examination. The effect of external examinations on the curriculum of the secondary school had been a matter for growing concern. The influential HMI Report, *Aspects of Secondary Education(1979)*, noted some of the effects they had perceived in their survey of secondary schools:
"...the effect of the dominating pursuit of examination results was to narrow learning opportunities, especially where work was concentrated on topics thought to be favoured by examiners. Sustained exposition by the teacher, and extensive note-taking by the pupil tended to limit oral work; this was especially likely to happen when the attainment of candidates had made them borderline performers ... In at least one-fifth of the schools the demands of public examinations appeared to be an important factor in the impoverishment of reading, with the least able pupils suffering most..."
Such observations were not new. In 1964 the Lockwood Committee on the examining of English Language had stated: "We have considered very seriously whether we should advise the cessation of these examinations for educational reasons ... we have come very near that conclusion." The Bullock Report had considered that English needed a "wider and more flexible range of assessment than most other areas of the curriculum" and had advocated "an increase in school-based assessment with external moderation."

CSE was one of the most important factors in changing the face of the examination system. It not only widened the target group for public examining but also:
"employed a much wider range of techniques of examining and assessing

25

than had been the norm in GCE and hence brought a wider range of skills and abilities into the net of assessment; in particular, the participation of the candidate's own teacher in the process of assessment became common along the lines of the Norwood Committee's recommendations. This participation was at its greatest in Mode 3 examinations, where the department or even the individual teacher devised the syllabus and scheme of examination and carried out the assessment, subject only to moderation by the CSE board." (Nuttall,1984)

The approaches used in CSE influenced GCE, where Mode 3 examinations and coursework-based assessment also began to appear. It was often English teachers who pioneered these developments; according to Desmond Nuttall, "NATE and LATE led the way". In West Yorkshire, however, it was English O Level which led CSE, with the introduction of 100% coursework schemes by the Joint Matriculation Board.

Continuous assessment based on coursework has enabled students to be assessed on their optimum achievements, in favourable conditions. It allows a much wider range of language uses to be assessed, and to be assessed in normal and supportive contexts. It enables work to be developed over time and revised; students are thus encouraged to become more reflective and to evaluate their own work more carefully. Some important recent developments have included a growth in individual or independent studies, where a student undertakes a substantial study on a topic of their own choice, using teachers as consultants. Under these kinds of assessment conditions, students have often exceeded their teachers' expectations, and their own. The careful and elaborate system of checks and controls developed by examining boards have ensured that work is carefully moderated and in many ways makes this form of examining more reliable and rigorous than conventional exam-hall approaches. Consortium moderation, where teachers meet regularly for trial marking sessions and to compare standards, has proved to be an important form of staff development. The experience of Mode 3 has greatly influenced GCSE; all of the GCSE boards now offer 100% coursework-based schemes alongside schemes based partly on end-of-course examinations.

Other developments which have been taking place have included the Records of Achievement movement, which has influenced practice in primary as well as secondary schools. Records of achievement began as a home-grown movement; a means of developing a school-leaving portfolio which would recognise a broader range of talents and achievements than would appear from examination results alone. Later examples focused on the involvement of pupils in their own assessment, and provided a full and positive description of a student's school experience. Parents were often involved in contributing to the records as well as being an audience for them. The movement was welcomed by employers and in 1984 the Government produced a policy statement which welcomed ROA and proposed that by 1990 there should be arrangements to allow every school-leaver to have such a record. But in 1989 the Government went back on this decision. Many LEAs are convinced of the value of ROA and intend to continue their schemes despite the Government's change of policy.

At primary level, there have been considerable developments in the observationally based recording of children's progress and development in language in particular. Though the original examples of this kind of development tended to be based on checklists, which were cumbersome to use and which were often over-prescriptive, later developments, such as the Primary Language Record (CLPE/ILEA) have used a combination of different and more open structures for observing and recording children's language and literacy development. Some of these techniques are familiar from classroom based research and case-study work (observation diaries, language and literacy "conferences" with children), while others reflect developments in psycholinguistics (error analysis). Approaches like this also enable teachers to observe children's individual strengths and needs and to take into account a wider range of achievements - for instance, the progress of bilingual children in all the languages in which they are literate.

Finally, the graded test movement, though very different in many respects from the other developments mentioned, is nevertheless, like them, an approach to assessment which began as a grass roots movement (among modern language teachers). It has since been taken up and developed by LEAs who have perceived it as a way of motivating secondary school students in the short term, and of providing modular qualifications.

The characteristic of graded tests, which are criterion-referenced tests in a progressive sequence, is that individuals should theoretically be able to work through them at their own rate, accumulating credits as they pass. This presents organisational difficulties, since individuals may be proceeding at very different rates, and the implications for comprehensive schools, especially for the grouping of students, would seem to be serious. English teachers, who have done so much to develop common courses for their students at 16+, have argued strongly against this form of assessment, on the grounds that it would lead to the premature categorisation of students, and thus to disaffection and disillusion, and also that it rests on the incorrect assumption that skills in language can be separately and precisely defined and then tested out of context. But the notion that it should be possible for students to proceed at their own pace up through a series of clearly defined levels and differentiated assessment tasks has obviously had an influence on the design of National Curriculum and has also opened the way to grouping by attainment level rather than by age.

What all these developments, even the graded test movement, have in common, is a much greater involvement of the teacher in assessment. The new emphasis is on broader-based and teacher-conducted assessment, which can sample children's achievements in a range of contexts, and involve children much more positively in their own assessment. This emphasis has created more flexible courses, enabled a much higher percentage of children to gain qualifications (about 80% or 90% of 16 year olds can expect to achieve a grade at GCSE), and has enabled assessment to be more diagnostic and detailed. It has also enabled complex skills and qualities to be assessed through holistic methods.

But alongside these developments has gone an increasing government emphasis on accountability and on the need for tighter central control of the education system, first through the monitoring machinery provided by the APU, then through the emphasis on national criteria for GCSE, and finally through the tight criterion-referenced model of the National Curriculum, which ties assessment down to sets of discrete objectives. The actual assessment of the National Curriculum will be done by teachers - both the internal assessment, and the external assessment through the SATs - but the constraints of the assessment model will mean that there is very little room for manoeuvre or for the kinds of broader goals mentioned above.

Patricia Broadfoot, in her book *Assessment, Schools and Society* explained this apparently paradoxical situation. She pointed out that the trend towards teacher-controlled assessment created problems of control of the system itself, and suggested that accountability measures would be likely to increase in response to the devolution of the day-to-day responsibility for assessment. She expressed this relationship in a diagram, which shows an "increasingly overt emphasis on accountability in proportion to the decline of various degrees of control on pupil certification... A consideration of contemporary trends in accountability does seem to emphasise that the diagonal in (the figure) is a constant, in which any decline in external control on one axis is likely to be made up by a corresponding increase in external control on the other".

28

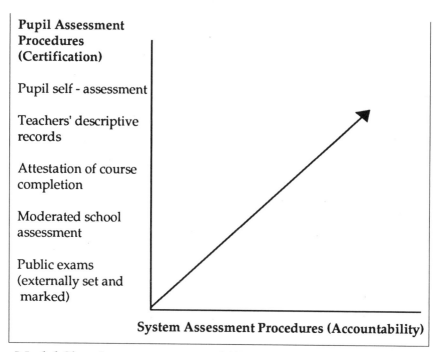

Pupil Assessment Procedures (Certification)

Pupil self - assessment

Teachers' descriptive records

Attestation of course completion

Moderated school assessment

Public exams (externally set and marked)

System Assessment Procedures (Accountability)

Model Showing overt accountability procedures as a function of declining public control of certification procedures *

The National Curriculum which puts the whole task of assessment - both 'internal' and 'external' - into the hands of teachers while simultaneously constituting a major accountability exercise, is an excellent, perhaps an ultimate, example of this proportionate relationship.

* From *Assessment Schools and Society* by Patricia Broadfoot, Methuen, 1979.

GOOD PRACTICE IN ASSESSMENT IN ENGLISH

The last section dealt briefly with some of the positive developments that have taken place in the field of assessment over the last twenty years. This section will continue that theme, firstly by reviewing those developments in the assessment of English and language that can be regarded as landmarks, and, secondly, by identifying some of the key principles that lie behind good practice in assessment.

A REVIEW OF PAST ACHIEVEMENTS IN THE ASSESSMENT OF ENGLISH AND LANGUAGE

This review of past achievements is in no sense intended to be a complete history. It is merely a summary of some of the important work which formed the background to more recent developments and which, whether consciously or not, such developments reflect.

1. The ending of the assessment of English grammar

The many arguments that had surrounded the assessment of English grammar in public examinations in the post-war period were finally laid to rest in 1964 by the Lockwood Report **Examining English Language**. Grammar questions had been a feature of the School Certificate in English and of the O Level English Language examination which replaced it, but there were many doubts about their value. The Lockwood Committee considered all the elements of English Language O Level and, as they reported, came near to recommending the complete abolition of the examination on the grounds that it had led to much bad practice. Eventually, however, they recommended only the discontinuation of the grammar questions on the grounds that "they serve no useful educational purpose and indeed have a bad effect on teaching." They considered that the skills such questions tested bore little relation to candidates' ability to write or understand English and concluded that the ability to write could best be assessed through the direct assessment of writing. They also considered that the grammar questions did "great harm" in that they perpetuated misleading notions of correctness which bore no relation to usage and which led pupils to "adopt a form of examination room English instead of seeking to express appropriately what they have to say." The Report led to widespread changes in the examining of English at O Level.

30

2. The use of multiple impression marking

The use of multiple impression marking for the assessment of children's writing was introduced into the eleven plus examination by Wiseman in 1949. (Before this method was introduced the marking of the essay had been by a method that involved error-counting). In the mid sixties, James Britton, Nancy Martin and Harold Rosen of the London Institute of Education used this work as a precedent whenthey conducted a study of the multiple impression marking of O Level English composition for the Schools Council (Schools Council Examinations Bulletin No.12, 1966). The marking of O Level composition was at that time generally carried out by individual markers using protocols - sample scripts giving examples of compositions worthy of 80%, 60%, and so on.

The Institute's study of multiple impression marking was carried out in seven schools over a period of a year, and revealed major gains in reliability over official marking procedures, together with some gains in validity. It showed that two markers were sufficient to account for most of the gains, though the addition of a third marker also increased the reliability of the assessment to some extent. Since this study, which was described in the British Journal of Educational Psychology as "a model of research in educational measurement", multiple impression marking has become a standard means of assessing written expression and has also been widely used in other contexts, such as oral assessment.

3. The assessment of comprehension as a unitary process

Work done by the London Association for the Teaching of English in the early 60s on assessing reading comprehension led to an "experimental paper" being offered by the London Board. The work involved attempts to assess a candidate's central understanding of the passage to be read. Instead of a series of separately scored questions testing comprehension of discrete elements of the passage, the method developed used a series of questions which were interconnected, and a marking scheme which was flexible enough to allow any answer which revealed understanding of the central points of the passage to be given extra weighting. This work also led to the inclusion of creative writing, as well as factual writing, in the choice of passages for comprehension.

Later developments in the examining of comprehension saw the advent of multiple choice comprehension at O Level English Language, and its subsequent rejection by teachers, who argued that comprehension as a unitary process could not be assessed by this atomistic and mechanistic method, or by an approach which allowed no room for candidates to express their understandings in their own words.

Subsequently the Schools Council "Effective Use of Reading" Project (Lunzer and Gardner 1979) attempted to identify measurably different subskills in comprehension, and found they could not do so. They identified instead only one general aptitude which they described as "the pupil's ability and willingness to reflect on whatever it is he is reading".

4. Error analysis

Early work on the analysis of miscues in reading by Kenneth and Yetta Goodman and Carolyn Burke in the early 60s in the USA has influenced all subsequent work on the assessment of reading. Goodman's 'Miscue Inventory' provides a basis for the analysis of all the types of error that readers make when reading aloud. The method enables positive miscues (e.g.intelligent substitutions) to be noted, as well as those miscues which are holding up understanding. The effect of this work has been to lead to a revaluation of the role of error in learning. Instead of being regarded as wholly negative phenomena, errors are regarded as information and as "a window on the reading process," since they often reveal the nature of a learner's theories about what readers have to do.

Subsequently, Mina Shaughnessy used similar insights to analyse the errors of Basic Writing students on access courses in New York. Shaughnessy's students were generally older students or adults with a history of failure in the education system; many of them were black or bilingual. Shaughnessy described their experience of writing in school in a passage that deserves to be remembered:
"Most damaging of all, they have lost confidence in the very faculties that serve all language learners: their ability to distinguish between essential and redundant features of a language left them logical but wrong; their ability to draw analogies between what they knew of language when they began school and what they had to learn produced mistakes; and such was the quality of their instruction that no one saw the intelligence of their mistakes or thought to harness that intelligence in the service of learning."
(Shaughnessy, 1977)

In the field of teaching English as a Second Language, Selinker, Pitt Corder and others used error analysis to examine the patterns of error made by

32

students at different stages of learning English, and found that there was a tendency for different stages to be marked by different types of error. Error analysis helps teachers by enabling them to adopt a diagnostic approach to error and thus to learn more about a student's understandings. What all such analysis demonstrates is that error is an integral part of learning, and that in favourable conditions, with support and feedback, learners do begin to self-correct, so that their language use shows a "gradual approximation towards correct forms." (Holdaway, 1979)

5. Assessing Oracy

The inclusion of oral language in public assessment began on a large scale with CSE, where oral work was a compulsory element. This inclusion has been an important development, even though oral assessment is still the hardest to get right. Issues of context and bias are never far away when considering the assessment of talk. At best, oral assessment procedures try to reproduce natural contexts for talk (e.g group orals), or as in GCSE, enable oral assessment to be continuous so that the normal oral work of the English classroom (e.g. discussions of reading and of written work) can count towards the assessment. But there has been disappointingly little ground-breaking work done that is as interesting as, for instance, the Southern Examining Board's Oral Chemistry Test (Schools Council Examinations Bulletin 21, 1971), though the APU assessed oracy partly through scientific problem-solving, and there have been developments in cross-curricular task-based oral assessment in Further Education. The assessment of oracy in the primary school, where cross-curricular assessment will be easier to organise, may prove to be an important area of development in national curriculum assessment.

What most of these successful past developments in assessment have in common is their attempt to form a whole picture of students as language users, and a view of language processes as complex and unitary. The next section will consider further what are the principles behind good practice in the assessment of English, and will offer examples of this practice.

THE PRINCIPLES THAT INFORM GOOD PRACTICE IN ASSESSMENT

English teachers and teachers concerned with language in the primary school now have substantial experience of developing systems of record-

33

keeping and assessment which reflect good practice, take a broad view of achievement, are informative (for children, parents, other teachers, and wider audiences) and do not distort the teaching and learning process. This section attempts to spell out the principles behind such good practice in assessment, and to give examples of the excellent professional standards which have been established in this field, especially through the involvement of teachers in external systems of assessment.

1. The assessment of normal behaviour in favourable contexts

It is now generally accepted that the sampling of normal behaviour in favourable day-to-day contexts is likely to give a better and more reliable picture of a child or a student's capabilities as a language learner than that which emerges from a one-off assessment in an unfamiliar situation (e.g an exam hall). This is the principle that has informed the development of coursework-based assessment at all levels of the education system, and that also underlies the development of Records of Achievement. 'Favourable contexts' are those classroom contexts which enable children to produce their best work; they can be created by, for example, stressing the value of extended units of work, focusing assessment on the process of learning as well as on end product, and developing tasks that seem likely to produce good writing or talk. Some kinds of assignments (e.g autobiography) tend to enable children to write more freely, authoritatively and well. These kinds of factors and their effects on children's performance need to be recognised in any system of assessment. The establishment of 100% coursework as a normal means of examining in GCSE demonstrates how far this principle has been generally accepted by the assessment community.

2. The importance of assessment across a range of contexts

This principle is linked to the previous one; it again stresses the role of context in determining performance. But the notion of a 'range of contexts' emphasises the fact that performance may vary in different kinds of contexts and that different kinds of tasks call for different skills. Just as in real life we use language for a variety of purposes, so in school different tasks call for the use of different language resources. The APU found strong evidence for task-specific features in the writing performance of eleven year olds, and in language performance generally. This finding "emphasises the limitations of a 'skills mastery' approach to writing performance, when the issue is the more complex one of context-of-use." (APU Primary Survey Report, 1982). The concept underlying the forms of

34

assessment they developed was that of a range of tasks to which pupils were invited to respond.

Most coursework-based assessment has the advantage of enabling performance to be assessed in a range of contexts. In the USA one recent development in the assessment of writing which reflects this principle is a form of coursework assessment known as 'portfolio assessment', which is now beginning to be used at all levels of the education system and across the whole curriculum. A recent study (Simmons, 1990) has shown that the weakest writers are enabled to demonstrate far more of their potential on portfolio assessment than on a conventional timed test, and that they also spend as much time on their portfolio assignments, write at as much length, and cover almost as many modes of discourse as the highest scoring students.

3. The assessment of process as well as product

When teachers switch their focus from the end product of a piece of learning to the actual process of learning, they form a fuller picture of the child as a learner, and are in a better position to intervene intelligently and to support children's learning helpfully. Assessment needs to reflect this growing emphasis on the process of learning, and has begun to do so through (at primary level) observationally-based records such as the Primary Language Record, which provides frameworks both for day-to-day observations, and for occasional in-depth analyses of children's language work. The value of children's self assessments and their involvement in the evaluation of their work are also signalled in the PLR, and are an important part of a process-oriented approach to assessment.

There is room for further development in this area. The assessment of a child's writing might, for instance, take into account more of the discussion, research, drafting and editing that go into a long piece of work instead of focusing exclusively, as is often the case, on the final draft. The Cox Committee recommended that these process aspects of writing be part of teachers' internal assessments. Such an approach also enables the role that talk and reading can play in writing to be acknowledged and included in the assessment, and points the way to a more holistic kind of assessment across all the language modes.

4. The holistic assessment of complex processes

Attempts to measure achievement in language analytically have increasingly come to appear less convincing because of the growing recognition that the processes to be assessed are complex and that the analytic forms of assessment used are often too crude to be useful - word recognition tests, for instance, are now generally recognised as being inadequate tests of reading. The problem with analytic approaches to assessment in language is that they usually rest on inadequate models of language, and that they do not recognise that, even if it were possible to break language processes down in some way or to identify sets of sub-skills, what counts as competence is the way in which a reader or writer is able to orchestrate these skills in a particular performance.

The Working Party set up by the Secondary Examinations Council on GCSE English Literature found that they could not usefully identify "domains", or subsets of skills and competencies, needed in the subject because of the "complexity and interrelationship of the element of an individual reader's response to a text." They considered that it was "not possible to identify sub-sets of skills or content which could be perceived and assessed as separate elements" and considered that any assessment system based on such a model might "give rise to the fragmentation of this area of curricular experience and to a narrow approach to teaching." They added that "any construction of domains appeared to us to involve making quite arbitrary decisions as to what did or did not constitute valid approaches to or models of the subject." The model of assessment they did recommend was the rank-ordering of candidates across grades from A to F, and they identified the criteria which they thought should be instrumental in the awards of grades F and A. These were broadly descriptive and holistic criteria, which attempted an all-round description of the kinds of achievement represented in the work of candidates at these grades.

The Working Party rejected the notion of 'hurdle criteria' - a system in which all criteria must be achieved before a specific grade can be awarded. They argued that predetermined hurdle criteria were contrary to the principle of assessing postitive achievement. They recommend that assessment should always start with a response to the candidates' work and that "only after the work has been read, or seen, or heard as a whole, and in its own right, should examiners begin to match it up with their own expectations of what the particular text and the particular task might require in the way of response from a reader." Their whole report offers subtle and intelligent commentary on the place of criteria in assessment, and on the need for a flexible and holistic approach to the assessment of complex processes. Had its arguments been heeded by the Cox Committee, the National Curriculum might look very different.

5. The sharing of criteria with students

Though English/language is an area which is best assessed holistically, it is clear that in assessments, judgements are always based on broad criteria, such as those identified by the SEC Working Party. Such criteria might include:

- (in writing) how far a writer has a well-developed sense of a reader and of a reader's needs;
- (in discussion) whether a student takes account of the points of view of other members of the group;
- (in reading) whether children are using a range of strategies in reading a text aloud, or are over-reliant on one or two strategies;
- (in general) whether a student is able to plan an extended piece of work and organise the work and her/his own time effectively.

Where teachers are using such criteria in assessment it is important that, as far as possible, the criteria being used should be shared with children/ students. There are impressive examples of teachers introducing the criteria that will influence assessment of students, and discussing with them afterwards how far such criteria have been met. In this way, students' own self-assessments can also become more informed and reliable.

Where criteria for assessment can be shared, and the content of the work is negotiated with the learner, as in the long study or coursework project which is a feature of some coursework based exams, then the assessment process is opened up and students gain more control over their learning. The JMB Language in Use project, which carries 20% of the marks in the board's English Language A Level examination is just one example of such long studies.

It is also important that criteria are shared with all the interested parties to assessment - including parents, employers, receiving schools, colleges, and so on - so that they are in a better position to 'read' assessment information. But lists of discrete criteria such as the National Curiculum provides are not likely to provide a helpful focus for communication between teachers and parents - as the Cox Committee suggested, assessment information will need to be set in context and presented in words rather than numbers to be truly informative.

6. The inclusion of pupils' self-assessment

Children and students can be involved in their own assessment in a number of ways. At the simplest level, they can keep records of their own reading, writing, and even perhaps their oral work, through simple dated lists and diaries. They can keep journals which serve as a commentary on their reading experiences, or which give a background to their finished writing. In discussions with teachers, which are recorded, they can be invited to comment on their own progress and on their strengths and needs, and periodically review their own work. They can be invited to reply to teachers' written comments on their work. And finally they can be given the opportunity to record their own assessments of their work, which can then become part of any summative assessment.

The DES policy statement on Records of Achievement recommended that the processes of assessing and recording should involve the pupil, and this has stimulated a great deal of work on self-assessment. Great care is needed to avoid self-assessment becoming a bland or routine exercise to be gone through, but some examples exist which show students taking over more responsibility for the evaluation of their own work and, in the process, becoming more reflective. It is clear that this development underpins much effective learning.

One example of such processes being incorporated into GCSE is the Leicestershire Mode 3 Drama syllabus, where students' self assessment is integral to the assessment. As part of the assessment students present an evaluation of the effectiveness of their work, which may be written, taped, or represented diagrammatically, and which should reveal "the degree to which the student has matched his/her own intentions".

Most teachers who have worked with pupils on self-assessment of any kind have found pupils' comments constructive and illuminating, and have also been impressed with the effects on pupils' confidence and their involvement in their own learning.

7. Equality in assessment

Finally, assessment practices need to take into account issues of equal opportunities. The danger of bias and discrimination in assessment was discussed in the ABC; any assessment scheme needs to be reviewed so that possible sources of bias can be identified and avoided. But it also needs to be borne in mind that unless pupils have equal access to the curriculum, they cannnot have equal treatment under *any* assessment scheme. Syllabuses and schemes of work always need to be carefully reviewed to make sure that they are accessible to all the students. One of the advantages of coursework-based assessment is that it allows for this kind of consideration to be taken into account far more easily, and enables both the content of the course and the assessment to be less biased than external assessment - which is designed for so-called "normal populations" - often is.

Many of the examples of good practice in assessment in English that have been described in this section necessitate the involvement of the teacher in the assessment process. The parallel need, therefore, for the comparison and evaluation of teachers' assessments, through a process of moderation, must also be mentioned. The successful experience of secondary English teachers and examining boards in developing reliable systems of moderation has meant that a great store of expertise now exists on this subject. There are basically three kinds of moderation; statistical moderation, moderation by inspection, and group moderation. Statistical moderation is not a method that is suited to the assessment of coursework. Moderation by inspection, or by visiting moderators, is probably the predominant model at GCSE generally, and is the method now being adopted in part for national curriculum assessment. But TGAT had favoured group moderation, which requires every teacher to be both an assessor of her/his own pupils and a moderator of someone else's, and which has been an important and ongoing form of inservice education for many teachers.

Secondary teachers feel positive about moderation, finding that it gives essential insights into how other teachers work, and into effective teaching strategies, as well as being a means of sharpening their own judgements and strengthening their educational thinking. Their substantial experience of investigating the basis of their judgements and of exploring the meaning of criteria in relation to actual examples of work will be invaluable in national curriculum assessment.

TGAT: PROBLEMS AND SOLUTIONS

When the TGAT Report appeared, it was generally welcomed by teachers and educationalists who saw it as a sophisticated and carefully balanced contribution to the literature of assessment. It did not advocate the kind of short sharp testing that many feared would be the consequence of national assessment. A number of its statements were reassuring; the often-quoted "Assessment should be the servant, not the master, of the curriculum" showed that the Task Group were aware of the pitfalls they had to negotiate and seemed to indicate that the place that assessment would have in the new system would be circumscribed.

Other features of the Report were also reassuring. The Task Group specifically recommended that up to Key Stage 4 - age 16 - the main purpose of assessment should be seen as formative and not summative: that is, its main purpose should be to inform teaching and provide information that would enable teachers to support the progress of learners more effectively. Secondly, the Task Group, while recommending that there should be external assessment at the four Key Stages, suggested that this was an area where substantial development was needed, and recommended that the assessment tasks developed should be as close to good classroom practice as possible. Thirdly, they placed as much emphasis on internal, or teacher assessment, as on external assessment, and spent a good deal of time discussing how the two kinds of assessment could be given equal status in the system. And finally they proposed that group moderation, which had been such an effective way of arriving at common standards in sixteen-plus examinations, as well as an important source of professional development at that level, should be the way by which teachers' judgements and the outcomes of the new SATs were compared and combined.

It is true that some of the later TGAT Reports, where the Task Group tried to spell out how some of their proposals could be implemented, were worrying, especially in their rough and ready plans for the development of a complex system of criterion-referenced level-related assessment and their advocacy of expensive and ineffective cascade models of inservice. But the full implications of the TGAT Report were not actually revealed until the subject working groups started to issue their reports and put flesh on the bones of the TGAT model.

Since TGAT was published, therefore, two things have happened to call its original model into question. One has been the working out in detail of the original proposals by the curriculum working parties. Unlike other government reforms - of the Health Service, for instance - the full picture of what was being proposed for the education system did not become apparent for some time after the original announcement of changes planned, indeed not until some of the new system was already on the statute books. In the first stages, therefore, even those who felt some misgivings about the TGAT model were inclined to give the proposals the benefit of the doubt. Moreover, if the professionals had started to criticise the new system before it had been given concrete form they would certainly have been written off as Luddites and wreckers. It has only been as the working parties have reported, and in particular since the arrangements for National Curriculum assessment have begun to be firmed up, that the flaws in the original conception have become glaringly obvious.

The second development that has compromised the TGAT proposals has been the way in which its vision of an assessment system has been revised by the Schools Examination and Assessment Council, which was charged with the task of interpreting its proposals. Little by little - with the downgrading of teachers' internal assessments, the disproportionate sums made available for SATs and the lack of resources to develop and disseminate good models of internal assessment, the ruling that where SAT results differ from internal assessments, the SAT results should be preferred, the reduction of the concept of moderation to a "court of appeal", instead of a real opportunity for professional (and system) development - the potential of the original TGAT proposals has been lost. In their place we are being presented with a cut-price version of their system, which looks more and more like a large-scale exercise in accountability and less and less like a true national system of assessment.

Moreover, some of TGATs original concerns about assessment in the primary school have been ignored altogether; subject working parties have reported without any reference to each other and there has been no attempt to coordinate their proposals or to mitigate the effects on the primary school of an essentially subject-based secondary school curriculum and system of assessment. The Frankensteinian consequences of this are becoming unignorable, and most people now realise that the demands on primary schools of this inappropriate model must somehow be alleviated. Yet the only support that has so far been offered to primary teachers by SEAC, the widely criticised pack on teacher assessment, has realised some of the worst fears about the invasiveness of assessment in the new system.

It is now possible to analyse in more detail the problems presented by the TGAT model of National Curriculum assessment, and to begin to suggest some tentative solutions. The one solution that is no solution at all, except perhaps in the short term, is that which has actually been announced by the Secretary of State; that in the primary school, and in particular at Key Stage One, there should be a simple mathematical reduction in the requirements of the system, with only the core subjects, being formally assessed. What is needed now is not an administratively feasible way of *managing* National Curriculum assessment on the existing model, but a change in the model itself. A national system of assessment is needed which draws on the very impressive examples of good practice in assessment that have been quoted in this document, and which meets the public demands that will be made of it in an educationally valid way.

This section begins with a detailed critique of the TGAT ten-level, criterion-referenced model of assessment, as it looks now that it is being interpreted in practical terms, and then moves on to consider some of the possible practical solutions to what is now visibly becoming, for the education profession and the government alike, a monstrous problem.

PROBLEMS OF THE TGAT MODEL

1. The ten-level model

TGAT's ten-level model has inherent in it particular dificulties, which will probably only become completely apparent when teachers begin to apply it in practice, and parents become aware of the effects on their children of this kind of crude grading. For English teachers, one of the most serious drawbacks of the ten-level model is that it enforces an unproblematic linear model of development on a language learning process which is, as the Cox Committee pointed out, often recursive, with children frequently revisiting earlier learning, and not progressing in a sequence of neatly ordered steps.

But there are problems for any subject in a model of assessment which tries to define levels of attainment independently of age - and this is what the national curriculum aims to do. Though there are guidelines as to the age at which most children may be expected to reach a particular level, with each level corresponding to roughly two years of progression in school, the TGAT commitee made clear that once the system was in place it should not be seen as closely age-related. The levels themselves, in other words, should eventually become the main point of reference, rather than what we know about age-appropriate learning, or stages of development.

The fact is that we do need to take development into account when we are considering children's learning. A very able seven year old cannot be regarded as the equivalent of an average fourteen-year old even if their attainment levels are similar. Children approach their learning very differently at different ages, and their experience as learners is different at these ages. A system of levels which takes no account of these fundamental differences will not help teachers to help children. The desire to develop an abstract ideal of progression misled the TGAT committee and caused them to ignore important evidence about how children actually learn and develop as learners.

2. Problems of criterion-referencing

Some of the problems to be anticipated from a criterion-referenced system of assessment on the scale that is now emerging were mentioned in the ABC section, and there are others also which need to be taken into consideration at this juncture. The major difficulties which we may expect to face in trying to implement such a system are the following:

a) As already explained, criterion-referenced assessment is inextricably linked with educational objectives-setting, and is thus designed to drive the curriculum. In English, this has set up a tension between the ostensible curriculum (the programmes of study) and the actual curriculum objectives contained in the attainment targets. The dangers that this objectives-based system may lead to, of a curriculum shrinking to what is to be assessed, are clear.

b) Evidence in Scotland and England at 16+ exists to show that where criterion-referencing has been introduced as the basis of an large-scale system of assessment it has not worked out well. The need to specify criteria in detail can lead to a fragmentation of a subject into small assessable elements, and the consequent loss of what Desmond Nuttall has called the "high-level and integrating objectives" which are actually the aspects of achievement that it would be most important to assess.

Furthermore, where there have been attempts before to link criteria with grades (or 'levels') these have had to be abandoned (as in the GCSE experiment with grade-related criteria) or greatly adapted (as in the case of the Scottish review of Standard Grade Assessment). In 1985 Dr Peter Martin, the Director of the criterion-referencing project at Jordan Hill College, Scotland, referred to grade-related criteria as "a bastard form of norm-referencing". His conclusions were that "Grade-related criteria should be abandoned altogether. They are an unhappy hybrid". The Times Educational Supplement described grade-related criteria as offending purists, experts, and teachers alike.

c) The criteria represented by the statements of attainment of the national curriculum are not based on sound evidence of what children can do at different ages and stages; they represent a mixture of what the curriculum working parties *thought* was likely to represent the typical achievements of a particular age group, and what we might term 'pious hopes' - notions of what children *ought* (according to the working parties) be able to do at these levels. The second supplementary report of the TGAT admitted that this would be the case, and that the system would not "depend on empirical evidence of a particular linear or other pattern of learning for its initial construction, although the definitions of the levels may need to be reviewed in individual cases in the light of information about the actual distribution of pupils' performance when the national curriculum and assessment system are in operation". They acknowledged that this was a "rough and ready" way of doing things; one can only agree.

d) Finally, and perhaps most importantly, many of the problems of criterion-referenced assessment relate to the question of how the criteria for assessment are developed, and who is involved in the development. It might have been possible to have worked in a consultative way towards sets of criteria that would have been generally accepted. This would have been an important piece of development from which we could have learnt a great deal. But the way the government has actually chosen to arrive at the criteria, through the off-the-cuff and uncoordinated recommendations of unrepresentative working parties working under great pressure, has resulted in a general sense that this system is being imposed on the schools for reasons that have much to do with political control and little with educational reform. At primary level, the predominance of secondary educationalists and academics in the working parties has led to a fragmented primary curriculum and to assessment demands which are generally recognised as unrealistic and excessive.

3. Problems of reporting the assessments

The criterion-referenced nature of the model is going to come up against real political hurdles when it comes to questions of reporting the results of assessment. It is clear that the only satisfactory ways of reporting the results of criterion-referenced assessment is through profile reporting. Because criteria are all different and are in no way equivalent to one another they cannot be added together, or summarised, without losing their meaning completely. Dr Peter Martin has referred to the "aggregation superstructure which destroys the descriptive power of the assessments". Where there are a plethora of criteria, there may be pressure to limit the number of criteria that are needed to achieve a particular level (the so-called 50% rule in maths and science) yet it is hard to see how these kinds of revisions can be implemented without compromising the basis of criterion-referenced assessment.

Moreover, criterion-referencing is not a suitable basis for a system of assessment where results are aggregated, presented in tables, and used in statistical exercises - which this is the usual kind of demand that is made on public assessment.

4. Problems of combining formative, summative and evaluative assessment.

The Task Group on Assessment and Testing attempted to create a system of assessment which would meet the needs both of formative and of summative and evaluative assessment. The means by which it hoped to reconcile these purposes was its ten-level model of assessment which it hoped would be used both as a guide to children's progress for the purposes of informal assessment and as a basis for arriving at judgement of overall achievement and reporting those achievements to parents, governors and LEAs. "We judge that an assessment system designed for formative purposes can meet all the needs of national assessment before 16".

It seems clear that this compromise is unlikely to work: formative and summative assessment cannot easily draw on the same information because their needs are very different and, where there is a conflict, it will always be the needs of summative and evaluative assessment that prevail. This is in fact the case with the ten-level model itself which is far more suited to the needs of summative assessment, with its emphasis on numerical grades, than it is to the needs of formative assessment, which ought to be more detailed and qualitative in its descriptions of progress.

We have already seen, in the developments across the country since the shape of the new system began to be clear, a disturbing tendency to 'place' children in relation to the levels, and to gear day-to-day recording to the levels of attainment. The effects on children of this kind of labelling, with what it is likely to lead to in the way of lowered expectations and depressed motivation, are to be feared. The effects of it on young children, who have hardly begun to make their way in the system, many from unprivileged homes, could be devastating. When summative measures are made the yardstick for formative assessment and recording, all it means is that children are given the opportunity to fail daily.

5. The problem of the SATs

At the time of writing, teachers' reactions to the experience of trying out the draft SATs for Key Stage One are beginning to be heard. Unsurprisingly, many teachers are finding the assessment tasks unworkable. The major practical problem is classroom management. One head teacher stated that "pilot tests had distressed her children and overwhelmed her teachers. The teachers had been expected to complete 176 different assessments for each of the sixty pupils being tested." (*The Guardian*, June 1st.) The NFER SAT contained 223 assessments.

It is important to stress that these difficulties are not attributable to the SATs so much as to the model of assessment, based on TGAT, that the education system has now to try to implement. One American visitor, who observed some of the SATs in action, has described the National Curriculum Attainment Targets as a "book-keeping nightmare" and has commented on the fact that the problems encountered by teachers in administering the SATs are a direct result of "the excessive detail of the curriculum and consequently the assessments".

6. Problems relating to equal opportunities

Finally, though the TGAT Report paid lip-service to equal opportunities, touched on questions of race and gender, and recommended that SATs developers should take questions of bias into account in developing their assessment tasks, it did not consider sufficiently how the system it was recommending might affect children from minority groups. It is true that a half-hearted recommendation suggested that some seven year olds might achieve better if they were assessed in first language rather than through the medium of English but, as Sibani Raychaudhuri pointed out recently (Raychaudhuri, 1990), it is pointless to suggest that assessment

46

should be in first language if the national curriculum makes no provision at all for learning in first language - and this is the effect of the emphasis on English in the National Curriculum, as the chapter on Bilingual Children in the Cox Report made clear.

This lack of careful thought about the effects of national assessment on children who are vulnerable in the system, and whose true ability is not always revealed by conventional measures of achievement, marks all subsequent developments from TGAT. In the zeal to create an internally self-consistent model of progression, the Task Group, and all subsequent groups charged with the interpretation of the model, have failed to consider whether such a system is likely to better or worsen the situation of children who are already at a disadvantage in the system. Evidence that reaches back to the days of the eleven plus (Pidgeon 1970) suggests that their situation is unlikely to be improved by the constant pressure to assess on essentially normative criteria that the TGAT model leads to.

Unless changes can be made to the new system of national curriculum assessment it seems likely that its effects on the education system will be negative in the extreme. Its effects on teachers' morale are already observable; no Saatchi and Saatchi campaign is likely to be able to sell this system to the profession, especially in the primary school. This is particularly unfortunate since much professional reaction to the national curriculum itself, as opposed to the system of assessment, has been favourable. Teachers have welcomed the guidance that curriculum documents have provided, and there have been in many staffrooms the kind of ongoing curriculum discussions that lead to real improvements in teaching and learning. The response of primary and English teachers to the Cox Report, and in particular to the actual curriculum frameworks presented in the programmes of study, has been generally positive, and where there have been points of difference it has been possible to argue them fruitfully.

In conclusion then, this section will consider what are the possible solutions to the problems presented by the TGAT model and by the system of national curriculum assessment which is resulting from it.

WHERE DO WE GO FROM HERE?

1. The need for an effective critique

Over the last few months there has been a surprising lack of effective critiques of national curriculum assessment (Ted Wragg's column on Mad

Curriculum Disease is an honourable exception). There is a need, now that the shape of the national curriculum is clearer, for professional associations to begin to look more closely at the likely effects of this system of assessment on the education system and particularly on primary schools. There is also a need for more information to be made publicly available about the reservations many educationalists now feel in relation to national curriculum assessment. Few parents realise the implications of the system that is on the horizon, and whereas the general public has some inkling of the drawbacks of the government's plans for the Health Service, not many people realise what is wrong with its education plans. There is also, of course, a need for the proposal of positive alternatives to these plans.

2. A review timetable

The national curriculum should be regarded as a first draft, and there should be immediate pressure for its review. The English Working Group emphasised the need for their recommendations to be "proved in the classroom" and stressed that they might "in due course need to be revised following a careful evaluation of the results". Immediate provision should be made for this evaluation, and for the review of the whole structure of national assessment, which is generally acknowledged to be very seriously flawed. There is no need to assume that such a review would lead to "something worse" - one of the arguments for inaction. The whole national curriculum experience has been a learning experience for everyone in the English educational system, and we should try to build on this learning.

3. Formative and summative assessment

One of the most serious flaws in the new assessment system is the attempt to combine formative and summative assessment. This combination, as has already been argued, is not a happy one. The formative and summative purposes of the national system should be separated and, as TGAT originally recommended, there should be no summative assessment before the age of 16. Before this, reporting to parents could still take place at key stages and indeed more frequently, but reports would be descriptive or narrative in character - words, not numbers - and would be based on teachers' records and on portfolios of children's work. These reports would draw on the experience of Records of Achievement and on profile reporting such as the Primary Language Record. The need to keep a check on standards within the system could be met by a monitoring programme based on the work of the APU. In addition, a rolling inservice programme would enable teachers to develop their assessment skills by comparing their judgements with those of other teachers, and arriving at common understandings of progress and development in particular curriculum areas through a process of moderation. The SATs might have a limited role to play within these programmes.

4. A new interpretation of criterion-based assessment

The work of the SEC Working Party offers the best way out of the problem of criterion-referencing. An interpretation of criterion-referencing should be arrived at which would ensure that criteria would inform assessment without dominating it. Criteria should be restated as broad clusters of abilities, not as lists of discrete skills. Most importantly, criteria should be drawn from a careful analysis of children's actual work, and not from some abstract model of progression. During the actual assessment process, teachers should be expected to attend in the first instance to a child's work, and respond to her/his positive achievements, as well as relating this performance to sets of criteria. Criterion-referencing, interpreted in this way, could inform assessment and curriculum planning, and could helpfully indicate to pupils and parents what teachers' expectations are, without coming to govern the entire educational process.

5. A working group on the primary curriculum

The TGAT Report recommended that a working group should be established to coordinate subject proposals for assessment in the primary school. Without such coordination they foresaw the danger of primary school teachers being faced with a heavy burden of assessment (para.119). These predictions have been realised and there is now an urgent need to review the whole of the national curriculum proposals as they relate to the primary school. There should be immediate and concerted pressure for such a review from all concerned parties.

These suggestions are intended as starting points for discussion rather than as considered solutions to the problems that were outlined earlier. In any such discussion of the reform of the national curriculum it is likely that English teachers and advisers, and those concerned with Primary Language, will be centrally involved. Historically, their role in the development of the assessment process has been important, and their collective experience of assessment and of the arguments relating to assessment is now substantial.

This book is offered to them as a resource, in the hope that it will add to their expertise in this area, and contribute to their arguments.

BIBLIOGRAPHY

ASSESSMENT OF PERFORMANCE **Language Performance**
UNIT Department Of Education and
Science (1978)

ASSESSMENT OF PERFORMANCE **Language Performance in**
UNIT **Schools:**
Primary Survey (1980) Report
No.2, H.M.S.O. (1982)

BARRS, M. et al **The Primary Language**
Record Handbook
ILEA/Centre for Language in
Primary Education (1988)

BLACK, Harry **Assessment for Learning**
in Nuttall, Desmond L. (Ed),
Assessing Educational
Achievement. Falmer Press
(1986)

BLACK, P. & MARJORAM, T. **National and State**
Assessment in the U.S.A
Department of Education and
Science (1979)

BROADFOOT, Patricia **Assessment, Schools and**
Society
Methuen (1979)

BURSTALL, Clare & **Assessment: The American**
KAY, Brian **Experience**
Department of Education and
Science (1978)

COHEN, D. **Evaluating Standards: Is**
There a Way?
Mimeo, MacQuarry
University, Australia (1978)

COHEN, S. Alan

Tests: Marked for Life?
Richmond Hill, Ontario,
Scholastic (1988)

COX, C.B. & DYSON, A.E. (Eds.)

**Fight for Education: a black
paper**
Critical Survey special issue
(1969)

Black Paper Two
Critical Survey special issue
(1969)

Black Paper Three
Critical Survey special issue
(1971)

COX C.B. & BOYSON, Rhodes

Black Paper
M.T. Smith (1977)

DEPARTMENT OF EDUCATION
AND SCIENCE

**Aspects of Secondary
Education in England:**
A survey by H.M. Inspectors
of Schools (1979)

DEPARTMENT OF EDUCATION
AND SCIENCE

**Education in Schools: A
Consultative Document**
HMSO (1977)

DEPARTMENT OF EDUCATION
AND SCIENCE

A Language for Life
(The Bullock Report) HMSO
(1975)

DEPARTMENT OF EDUCATION
AND SCIENCE

English for ages 5 - 16
June (1989)

EISNER, Elliot W.

**The Art of Educational
Evaluation: a Personal View,**
Falmer Press (1985)

GIPPS, Caroline

A Critique of the APU in Nuttall, Desmond L.(Ed.) **Assessing Educational Achievement,** Falmer Press (1986)

GIPPS, Caroline, STEADMAN, S. BLACKSTONE, T. & STEIRER, B.

Testing Children: standardised testing in local education authorities and schools Heinemann Educational Books, (1983)

GLASER, Robert

Instructional Technology and the Measurement of Learning Outcomes: some questions American Psychologists (1963) 18pp 519-21

GOLDSTEIN, H.

Consequences of Using the Rasch Model for Educational Assessment British Educational Research Journal, 5, 2, pp 211-20 (1979)

GOODMAN, Yetta M & BURKE, Carolyn L.

Reading Miscue Inventory: Practice Analysis Manual. Procedure for Diagnosis and Evaluation. N.Y. Macmillan, 1972

GUPTA, Rajinder M. & COXHEAD, Peter (Eds.)

Cultural Diverstiy and Learning Efficiency: Recent Developments in Assessment Macmillan, (1988)

HARGREAVES, David H.

Improving Secondary Schools ILEA (1984)

HOLDAWAY, Don

Foundations of Literacy
Sydney, Australia, Ashton
Scholastic, (1979)

HOUSE, Ernest R.

**An American View of British
Accountability**
in Becher, T.& Maclure, S.
Accountability in Education
Windsor Berks. NFER (1978)

LABOV, William

**The Logic of Non-Standard
English**
in Williams, Frederick (Ed.)
Language and Poverty,
Chicago, Markham Publishing
(1969)

LAPOINTE, Archie E.

Testing in the U.S.A.
in Nuttall, Desmond (Ed.)
**Assessing Educational
Achievement,**
Falmer Press (1986)

LOCKWOOD COMMITTEE

**Report of a Working Party on
the School Curriculum and
Examinations**
Department of Education and
Science (1964)

LUNZER, Eric &
GARDNER, Keith (Eds.)

The Effective Use of Reading
Heinemann Education (1979)

MACINTOSH, H.G. &
HALE, D.E.

**Assessment and the
Secondary School Teacher**
Routledge and Kegan Paul
(1976)

MACLURE, Stuart

Introduction: Background to the Accountability Debate in Becher, Tony and Maclure, Stuart (eds.) **Accountability in Education** Windsor, Berks. NFER (1978)

MURPHY, Roger & TORRANCE, Harry

The Changing Face of Educational Assessment Milton Keynes, Open University Press (1988)

NATIONAL CURRICULUM TASK GROUP ON ASSESSMENT AND TESTING

A Report D.E.S., (1987)

NISBET, John

Procedures for Assessment in Becher, Tony and Maclure, Stuart (eds.) **Accountability in Education** Windsor, Berks. NFER (1978)

NUTTALL, Desmond

Will APU Rule the Curriculum Supplement to Education, 6th June pp1x-x (1980)

NUTTALL, Desmond

Assessing Educational Achievement Falmer Press (1986)

NUTTALL, Desmond

Doomsday or New Dawn? The prospects for a common system of examining at 16+ in Broadfoot, P.M. (Ed.) Selection and Certification and Control Falmer Press (1984)

NUTTALL, Desmond

National Assessment - Will Reality Match Aspirations? Text of a Paper delivered as part of the Conference Testing Times organised by Macmillan Education on March 8th ,1989 (1989)

NUTTALL, Desmond et al

Bera Policy Task Group on Assessment: Discussion Paper on National Curriculum Assessment . An unpublished paper, (1990)

PIGEON, D.A

Expectation and Pupil Performance Slough, NFER, (1970)

POPHAM, W.J.

Two-plus Decades of Educational Objectives International Journal of Educational Research 11 (1) pp 31-41 (1987)

PRING, R. & SELBY, C.

Draft Report on the American Visit Assessment of Performance Unit/Department of Education and Science,(1979)

RAYCHAUDHURI, Sibani

Children off the Edge: English in the National Curriculum. Language Matters, 1989 No. 3

RECORDS OF ACHIEVEMENT NATIONAL STEERING COMMITTEE

Records of Achievement: report January, (1989) D.E.S.

SCHOOLS COUNCIL EXAMINATIONS BULLETIN. NO. 12	Multiple Marking of English Compositions: An account of an experiment by James Britton et al. HMSO, (1966)
SCHOOLS COUNCIL EXAMINATIONS BULLETIN NO. 41	Review of Graded Tests by Andrew Harrison Methuen Educational, (1982)
SCHOOLS COUNCIL CSE: EXAMINATIONS BULLETIN NO. 21	An Experiment in the Oral Examining of Chemistry by P. Brown et al. Evans/Methuen, (1971)
SECONDARY EXAMINATIONS COUNCIL	Report of Working Party: English Literature (1986)
SHAUGHNESSY, Mina P.	Errors and Expectations: A guide for the Teachers of Basic Writing N.Y. Oxford University Press, (1977)
SIMMONS, JAY	Portfolios as large-scale assessment in Language Arts Vol 67 No. 3 March, (1990)
START, K.B. & WELLS, B.K.	Trends in Reading Standards Windsor, Berks. NFER (1972)
STIBBS, Andrew	Assessing Children's Language Ward Lock Educational/ NATE (1981)
WRAGG, Ted	Who put the Ass in Assessment? Times Education Supplement, 16 February (1990)

National Association of Advisors in English.

Aims

The association was formed in 1977 with the following aims:

1. To provide a forum for the exchange of views, information and experience relating to all aspects of teaching English to all age groups in local authority establishments;

2. To provide an organisation to discuss the promotion of policies for the development of teaching English;

3. To provide, as required, advice upon such policies or any other pertinent matters to other persons or bodies;

4. To make provision for representation on or to other bodies in furthurance of these aims;

5. To foster the interests of its members and help them where possible.

The existence of the Association has meant that the views of advisers have been represented in national discussions of important issues affecting the teaching of English. The term English is used here in its widest sense, covering all aspects of reading and language development at both primary and secondary level.

Activities

The Association provides opportunities for advisers to meet regularly to share concerns and ideas. Each member is linked with one of the regional groups represented on the National Committee, and these groups organise their own programmes. In addition, one-day national seminars are normally held three times a year in various locations to allow members to hear authorative speakers on matters of current concern. Her Majesty's Inspectors and other interested professionals are frequently invited to join in these meetings, and in the annual residential course/conference held in September. The Association's AGM is currently held during this event.

Members also benefit from the national and regional disribution and exchange of information and publications relevant to their subject areas. The Association has been involved in a number of regional and nationwide studies, curriculum projects and consultation exercises.

For further information, please contact:

Mr. I. G. Ball, Senior Adviser, English, Education Department, Avon House North, St. James Barton, Bristol BS 99 76B

The National Association for the Teaching of English

NATE represents the interests of those involved in the teaching of English.

Membership provides:

Free publications including 'English in Education'. NATENEWS and 'The English Magazine'

Locally based support groups

Annual national conference

Free advisory service

Guidelines on emerging national issues

For further details, contact:
NATE,
50 Broadfield Road,
Broadfield Business Centre,
Sheffield S8 0XJ

Telephone: (0114) 255-5419
         Fax: (0114) 255-5296